Stalin

PETER CHRISP

HODDER
Wayland

an imprint of Hodder Children's Books

© 2002 White-Thomson Publishing Ltd

Produced for Hodder Wayland by
White-Thomson Publishing Ltd
2/3 St Andrew's Place
Lewes
BN7 1UP

Other titles in this series:
Churchill
Kennedy
Hitler

Series concept: Alex Woolf
Editor: Nicola Edwards
Design: Derek Lee
Consultant: Professor Scott Lucas,
  University of Birmingham
Picture research: Shelley Noronha,
  Glass Onion Pictures
Map artwork: Nick Hawken
Proofreader and indexer: Alison Cooper

First published in Great Britain in 2002 by Hodder
Wayland, an imprint of Hodder Children's Books

British Library Cataloguing in Publication Data
Chrisp, Peter
  Joseph Stalin. – (20th century leaders)
  1. Stalin, Joseph, 1889-1945 2. Heads of state –
  Germany
  I. Title
  943'.086'092

ISBN 0 7502 35853

Printed in Hong Kong by Wing King Tong

Hodder Children's Books
A division of Hodder Headline Limited
338 Euston Road, London NW1 3BH

Picture acknowledgements: The publisher would like
to thank the following for permission to use their
pictures: All pictures are from the David King
Collection except p9 AKG London; pp5, 8, 29, 45,
46, 49 HWPL; 42, 51, 58, 59 Popperfoto.

Cover picture: Camera Press Ltd

Contents

CHAPTER ONE

The Young Stalin

A HARSH CHILDHOOD

Joseph Vissarionovich Dzugashvili, who later called himself Stalin (the 'steel one'), was born on 6 December 1878, in the little town of Gori, in Georgia, in the south-western corner of the vast Russian Empire.

The family spoke Georgian, and Joseph only learned to speak Russian at school, when he was eight or nine. He would always speak Russian with a strong Georgian accent, and never felt completely at ease when he was speaking his second language.

▼ Joseph Dzugashvili, in his mid teens.

It was a violent household, and Joseph was regularly beaten by his mother and his father, who was a drunkard. His parents also fought each other, quarrelling over the boy's future. His father was a shoe maker and mender, who expected his only child to follow the same trade. But his mother, who was very religious, hoped that Joseph might become a priest.

This harsh home life may have shaped the boy's character. According to a schoolfellow, Joseph Irimashvili, the young Stalin 'was incapable of feeling pity for man or beast'. Hana Moshiashvili, a friend of Stalin's mother, remembered him as 'an embittered, insolent, rude, stubborn child with an intolerable character'.

TEENAGE REBEL

Yet Joseph was also hard working and bright. At the age of 15, he was enrolled in the seminary (priests' training college) at Tiflis, the capital of Georgia. Training for the priesthood was the only form of further education open to a clever boy from a poor family. But, despite his mother's hopes, Joseph had no intention of becoming a priest. He was a rebel, who was often in trouble for reading 'forbidden books', such as Charles Darwin's scientific writings. Darwin's theory that humans had evolved from apes challenged the teachings of the Church. A classmate remembered him reading Darwin, and concluding, 'There is no God, they are deceiving us.'

Joseph also read an author whose theories were sweeping Russia and winning thousands of converts among the young - Karl Marx.

YOU SHOULD HAVE BEEN A PRIEST

In 1935, Stalin, by then the ruler of the Soviet Union, visited his mother, Ekaterina. The following conversation was recorded by her doctor.

Ekaterina: Joseph – who exactly are you now?

Stalin: Remember the tsar? Well, I'm like the tsar.

Ekaterina: You'd have done better to have become a priest.

▼ The German philosopher and political theorist, Karl Marx.

MARXISM

Karl Marx (1818–83) saw all history as driven by struggles between different classes. He predicted a coming clash between the proletariat (industrial working class) and the capitalists (property-owning class). Marx said that the working class would win, and would set up a new worldwide order based on communism (common ownership). Once private property had been abolished, everyone would be equal and there would be no more oppression or injustice.

Marx presented his theory (Marxism) as a way of explaining history. Yet Marxism was also like a religion: it claimed to be the only true path to follow, and promised to deliver happiness for all at some future date (see page 10). For Stalin, Marxism provided a new set of beliefs, replacing the Christian teachings he had rejected.

▶ Lenin (seated third from the left) with fellow Social Democrats in 1897. Lenin and the man to his left, Yuli Martov, would later become enemies, leading rival factions, the Bolsheviks and the Mensheviks.

STALIN THE MARXIST

After reading Marx, Stalin became a revolutionary, committed to bringing about the class clashes predicted by Marx. In 1898, he joined the Social Democratic Workers' Party, which had been formed by Russian Marxists. He saw no point in continuing his education and, in May 1899, he was expelled from the seminary for failing to sit an exam.

Among the Social Democrats, there was a big disagreement about how communism was to be achieved. The problem was the backwardness of the Russian Empire. Out of its population of 160 million, 130 million were poor peasant farmers. The industrial working class, which, according to Marx (see page 5), was supposed to bring about revolution, made up just 10 per cent of the population. Most workers were more concerned with getting a decent living wage than building communism. One group of Marxists believed that revolution would have to wait until the working class had grown much bigger, and become politically aware. They favoured creating a political party with many thousands of members, which would gradually win over the workers to communist ideals. At the right time, they said, history would bring about the revolution.

BOLSHEVIKS AND MENSHEVIKS

Vladimir Ilyich Lenin, a leading Social Democrat, did not want to wait this long. Lenin wanted to give history a push. In *What is to be Done?* (1902), he argued for the creation of a small disciplined party of professional revolutionaries. This party would act as a 'vanguard' or leading group of the working class, on whose behalf it would seize power. Lenin wrote, 'Give us an organization of revolutionaries and we shall turn Russia upside down.'

In 1903, this argument split the Social Democratic Party into two warring factions. The group led by Lenin was now known as the Bolsheviks (majority) while his opponents were called the Mensheviks (minority).

'LENIN'S LEFT LEG'

Admiring Lenin, Stalin became a Bolshevik. According to a fellow revolutionary, R. Arsenidze, Stalin 'worshipped Lenin, he deified [made a god of] Lenin. He lived on Lenin's thoughts, copied him so closely that we jokingly called him "Lenin's left leg".'

For eighteen years, Stalin was active in the revolutionary underground. He wrote and distributed political articles; helped to organize strikes and demonstrations; and he planned bank robberies, to raise money for the party. He also found time to marry, though his wife, Ekaterina, died in 1908, leaving him with a baby son, Yakov.

Stalin was arrested eight times for revolutionary activities, receiving sentences of imprisonment and exile. Between 1908 and 1917, he was to spend just one and a half years as a free man.

LENIN

'Lenin' was the adopted name of Vladimir Ilyich Ulyanov (1870–1924), the middle-class son of a Russian school inspector. He had a happy and uneventful early life until he was 17, when his older brother Sasha was hanged for his role in a plot to assassinate the tsar. This traumatic event turned the young Lenin towards revolutionary politics. With his dominant personality, immense will power and unshakeable self-belief, Lenin was to become a dynamic revolutionary leader.

▼ Stalin's police file of April 1910. He had just been recaptured by the police, following one of several escapes from exile.

7

CHAPTER TWO

Revolution

UPHEAVAL IN RUSSIA

The Bolsheviks' opportunity to seize power came with the First World War, which began in 1914. By the beginning of 1917, the war had brought Russia to a state of near chaos, with soaring inflation and food shortages.

In February 1917, the factory workers of Petrograd, the Russian capital, went on strike. There were riots and demonstrations, calling for peace and bread. The soldiers, commanded to restore order, mutinied and began to shoot their officers. On 2 March, the Tsar abdicated, and a new provisional government was set up, pledged to hold democratic elections.

The Bolshevik leaders played no part in this revolution. They were either abroad, like Lenin, or serving sentences of internal exile. When the new government freed political prisoners, the exiles, including Stalin, made their way as quickly as possible to Petrograd.

In the spring of 1917, the idea that the Bolsheviks might take power seemed incredible. They were a tiny party, with only 26,000 members. The Bolsheviks were just one of a number of revolutionary parties, and did not even control the Petrograd Soviet (council), set up to represent the revolutionary workers and soldiers. Most Bolsheviks thought that they should reunite with the Mensheviks and work with the provisional government.

▼ Lenin was able to sway crowds, using simple, direct and forceful speeches. Trotsky said that listening to Lenin was like watching a man 'striking a mighty blow with his hammer on the head of the nail.'

LENIN'S ARRIVAL

Everything changed on 3 April, when Lenin reached the capital by train from Switzerland. Immediately he called for the overthrow of the new government in the name of the proletariat. Lenin argued that a workers' revolution in Russia would be a spark, setting off similar revolutions throughout Europe. With his forceful personality, Lenin was able to get a majority of his fellow Bolsheviks to accept the new line.

GOVERNMENT FAILURES

The provisional government failed to solve any of Russia's problems. Instead of ending the war, it launched a new large-scale offensive, which was a disastrous failure. It was unable to supply food to the cities or to control the countryside, where the peasants began to seize the land for themselves.

BOLSHEVIK SUPPORT GROWS

As the only party opposed to the government, the Bolsheviks benefited from its failures. Membership rose quickly and, by October, the Bolsheviks had majorities in the Petrograd and Moscow Soviets (councils).

In July 1917, a former Menshevik called Leon Trotsky (1879–1940) joined forces with Lenin. Trotsky was a skilled organizer and a dazzling public speaker, who was soon second only to Lenin in the Bolshevik leadership. It was Trotsky who planned the details of the military uprising, which took place on 24–5 October 1917. Trotsky's Red Guards (armed workers, soldiers and sailors) seized key buildings in the city and arrested the provisional government. With hardly a shot fired, the Bolsheviks were in charge.

▲ In a 1920 painting by Boris Kustodyev, a giant Bolshevik carries a red flag – a symbol of revolution – through Petrograd, at the head of an invincible army of workers, sailors and soldiers.

1917: BEHIND THE SCENES

Stalin played a minor role in the events of 1917, but he was busy behind the scenes doing organizational work for the party. A Menshevik, Nikolai Sukhanov, recalled:

'Stalin... with his modest activity... produced, and not on me alone, the impression of a grey blur, dimly looming up now and then, and leaving no trace behind him. And that, really, is all that can be said of him.'

Smiling children stand
beside the smashed
statue of Tsar Alexander
III in Moscow. The Russian
monarchy, toppled in
February 1917, had gone
for ever.

LENIN TAKES CHARGE

'We are going to destroy and smash everything,' said Lenin after taking power, 'and on the ruins we shall build our temple! It will be a temple for the happiness of all!'

Destroying the old Russia was the easy part. Lenin would find it much harder to build his new communist paradise. The January 1918 election, which Lenin allowed to go ahead as planned, showed that he had little support in the country. Lenin decided to do away with free elections. Soon all political parties were banned except the Communist Party, as the Bolsheviks renamed themselves.

The most urgent task was to end the war. By 1918, German troops were so close to Petrograd that Lenin had to move the capital to Moscow. In March, the Germans agreed to peace, but at a heavy price. Russia had to give up vast territories. Lenin called this 'trading space for time'. He was still confidently expecting his revolution to sweep through Europe.

CIVIL WAR

It would take three years of bitter civil war before the Communists were secure. Ranged against them were various armies of anti-communist 'Whites' (white was a

▶ From his armoured train, Leon Trotsky (right, in train doorway) leads the Red Army to victory.

colour linked with purity, Christianity and monarchy), backed up by more than a dozen foreign states. The direction of the war was left to Trotsky, creator and leader of the new Red Army. Trotsky criss-crossed Russia in his armoured train, rushing from one front to another. Stalin also held military commands, on the southern front, where he frequently disobeyed Trotsky. This was the beginning of a lifelong feud between the two men.

FAMINE

Meanwhile, Lenin tried to impose a communist economy on the country. The free market was banned. Peasants, forbidden to sell their grain, were supposed to hand it over to the state, in return for manufactured goods, such as tools and clothes. However, the peasants refused to give up their grain, and there were too few factories to manufacture enough goods for the countryside. To feed the cities and the Red Army, the grain was seized by force. This system, called 'war communism', helped the Communists fight the civil war, but was finally a failure. The peasants stopped farming, and a terrible famine gripped the countryside. Millions starved, or survived by turning to cannibalism.

RED TERROR

From the beginning, the Communists used terror against their opponents. Their *Cheka* (secret police) was more ruthless than the tsarist secret police had ever been, with unlimited powers to shoot suspected 'class enemies'. The police journal *Red Sword* justified this use of terror:

'Ours is a new morality... For us everything is permitted, for we are the first in the world to raise the sword, not for the purpose of enslavement and oppression, but in the name of liberty.'

Discussing the killing of the Tsar and his family, Trotsky gave another reason for terror:

'[This was necessary] to give our own ranks a jolt, show them there is no going back. Ahead of us lies total victory, or total disaster.'

ДА
ЗДРАВСТВУЕТ АВАНГАРД
РЕВОЛЮЦИИ
КРАСНЫЙ ФЛОТ

▲ A heroic sailor in a 1919 poster honouring the Red Fleet. Two years later, the sailors at Kronstadt would rebel against the Bolsheviks.

PEASANT UPRISINGS

By late 1920, the Communists had won the civil war, but their ruthless methods had lost them the little support they had in the country. In 1920–21, the Red Army had to put down widespread peasant uprisings. In March 1921, there was a mutiny at the Kronstadt naval base. The sailors, mostly peasants, had been strong supporters of Lenin. Now they called for an end to the party's dictatorship and the return of a free market in the countryside. Trotsky crushed the mutiny with great bloodshed.

By now, it seemed highly unlikely that revolution would spread through Europe, as Lenin had hoped. The Communists were left feeling like a besieged army, menaced by internal as well as foreign enemies.

Lenin realized that his attempt to force communism on the peasants had failed. In March 1921, he announced the 'New Economic Policy', which allowed the peasants to sell produce once more in a free market. Lenin described this as a tactical retreat on the road to communism. It was unpopular with most party members, but Lenin told them there was no alternative. He said, 'So long as there is no revolution in other countries, only agreement with the peasantry can save the socialist revolution in Russia.'

'COMRADE CARD INDEX'

In April 1922, Lenin asked Stalin to become General Secretary of the Communist Party. As 'Gensek', he was responsible for party appointments and demotions and set committee agendas. Stalin seemed the perfect man for the job. He had a vast capacity for hard work and an excellent memory – characteristics which earned him the nickname 'Comrade Card Index'.

Gensek was just one of Stalin's roles. He was also a member of the Politburo (Political Bureau), the party's decision-making body. He was People's Commissar for Nationalities – the minister responsible for the state's non-Russian peoples – and he was chairman of the Orgburo (Organizational Bureau), the department which passed down Politburo orders to local party branches throughout the country.

▲ Although Stalin was little known to the public in 1922, his appointment as General Secretary gave him enormous power.

At the time, Stalin's new appointment as Gensek seemed unimportant, and solely to do with administration. The leaders believed that real power lay in the Politburo, where they argued over policy. Only Stalin realized that his new post could become a basis for future power. He would use it to promote his own supporters and build up a power base within the party.

A month after appointing Stalin as Gensek, Lenin suffered a stroke which partly paralysed him, and left him unable to speak. With Lenin ill, the other Politburo members were soon involved in a power struggle.

DESCRIPTION OF STALIN

John Reed was a US communist who settled in Russia, and got to know many of its leaders. In 1920, he said of Stalin: 'He's not an intellectual like the other people you will meet. He's not even particularly well-informed, but he knows what he wants. He's got will power, and he's going to be top of the pile one day.'

CHAPTER THREE

Stalin's Rise To Power

RIVALRIES

In 1922, the leading figures in the Politburo were Leon Trotsky and Grigori Zinoviev, party chief of Petrograd. As a speech maker, Zinoviev was second only to Trotsky, and he was world famous as president of Comintern, the Communist International (the international grouping of communist parties). The other Politburo members were Lev Kamenev, party chief of Moscow, and Nikolai Bukharin, economist and editor of *Pravda* (*Truth*), the party newspaper. All of these men seemed more important than Stalin, who was barely known outside the party.

Within the Politburo, there were bitter rivalries. Stalin and Trotsky had never got on. Kamenev and Zinoviev were close allies who feared Trotsky. Zinoviev, especially, detested Trotsky. Ambitious to lead the Communist Party, Zinoviev was jealous of Trotsky's prestige as organizer of the revolution and victor in the civil war. The easy-going Bukharin was the only one who got along with everyone else. They all felt intellectually superior to Stalin.

To the members of the Politburo, it was Trotsky, not Stalin, who looked like a possible dictator. Trotsky never hid his contempt for his colleagues; he had shown great

STALIN AT POLITBURO MEETINGS

Boris Bazhanov, Stalin's secretary in the 1920s, described Stalin's behaviour at Politburo meetings:

'He was mostly tongue-tied. He smoked his pipe and spoke very little... Stalin was not an educated man and my impression was that some of the more complicated questions of state were beyond him... Stalin had the good sense never to say anything before everyone else had his argument fully developed... he would then repeat the conclusions towards which the majority had been drifting.'

ruthlessness in the civil war; and he still led the Red Army.

To stop Trotsky, an alliance was formed by Zinoviev, Kamenev and Stalin. Zinoviev and Kamenev both felt that they were using Stalin. Kamenev described Stalin as 'just a small town politician' – a good administrator, but a man with no ideas or ambitions of his own.

▲ Stalin (left) with Zinoviev (right) and Kamenev (second right).

STALIN'S POPULARITY INCREASES

Although Stalin did not impress his fellow leaders, he was gaining in popularity among ordinary party members. Since 1917, membership had risen from 26,000 to over 500,000. Mostly poorly educated, the newcomers found the brilliant Trotsky an intimidating figure. Yet nobody felt inferior to Stalin, with his shabby clothes and thick Georgian accent. People appreciated the fact that he seemed never to forget a name or a face, and he soon gained a reputation as a good listener.

In 1922, Stalin used his position as Gensek and head of the Orgburo to appoint around 10,000 party officials in the provinces. These would be his main supporters in the coming struggle for power.

STALIN AND TROTSKY

Maria Yoffe, a friend of Trotsky's, contrasted the two men:

'[Stalin] behaved like an ordinary, pleasant fellow, extremely sociable and on friendly terms with everyone, but it was all phoney... Trotsky created an invisible barrier in his relations with others; he kept people at a distance... Trotsky's behaviour created the impression of arrogance.'

15

LENIN'S DISMAY

Meanwhile, Lenin was slowly recovering from his stroke. He determinedly taught himself to speak again and by October 1922 was ready to return to government.

Lenin was dismayed to see how the country had been run in his absence. He saw how powerful Stalin had grown, and he was worried by the ways in which he was abusing his power. He believed that the old Bolshevik revolutionary spirit was being strangled by a vast bureaucracy.

Before Lenin could do much about Stalin, he had a second stroke, on 13 December 1922. Stalin took charge of his medical treatment, and stopped him receiving newspapers, visitors or political information.

Although Lenin was a virtual prisoner, Stalin could not stop him leaving a 'political testament', a last statement to be delivered to the party on his death. Lenin wrote that Stalin had gained too much power, and that he was too rude and coarse. He suggested that the party find a way to remove Stalin from his post as Gensek.

A DANGEROUS TESTAMENT

Lenin made another slight recovery, and was planning to address the party congress in April. According to Trotsky, on 7 March 1923, Lenin's secretary Lidia Fotieva visited him and said, 'Ilyich [Lenin] does not trust Stalin. He wants to come out openly against him before the whole party. He is preparing a bombshell.'

Lenin never delivered his bombshell. Two days later, a third stroke finally robbed him of the power of speech. Lenin lived on for another eleven months, but his political life was over.

▼ Following Lenin's death, on 21 January 1924, Stalin had his coffin displayed in Moscow's Red Square. Tens of thousands of Russians came to pay their respects, despite the freezing temperatures.

The testament left by Lenin was still a dangerous weapon against Stalin. But when it was read out at a Central Committee meeting, Kamenev and Zinoviev defended Stalin from Lenin's criticisms. Trotsky, who was hopeless at political infighting, said nothing. According to a witness, Boris Bazhanov, 'One could read from his face that he regarded Stalin, Zinoviev, Kamenev... as inferior creatures with whom he would not stoop to tangle.'

Stalin had begun to create a personality cult of Lenin, who was now presented as the source of all wisdom. Stalin would always refer to himself as a 'Leninist', and would use Lenin's writings as a sacred text, to back up every political position he adopted. Petrograd was renamed Leningrad, and statues and vast posters of the dead leader appeared everywhere. Being turned into a cult would have horrified Lenin, who once said, 'Monuments only attract pigeons.'

THE CULT OF LENIN

Stalin organized a grand funeral service for Lenin, which he prevented Trotsky from attending by giving him the wrong date. Stalin made a speech with religious overtones:

'Leaving us, Comrade Lenin ordered us to hold high and keep pure the calling of a member of the party. We vow to thee, Comrade Lenin, that we will honour this, thy commandment.'

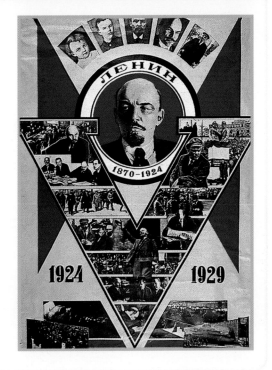

▶ A 1929 poster celebrates Lenin on the fifth anniversary of his death.

SOCIALISM IN ONE COUNTRY

One of Trotsky's points in *The Lessons of October* was that the revolution would perish unless it spread to the West. Stalin replied with a new idea, 'Socialism in One Country'. He said that Russia alone could build a communist society. In his memoirs, Petro Grigorenko, who was a young party member, remembered the impact of Stalin's idea: 'I read *Lessons of October*... I was uneasy. Could Trotsky possibly be right? Might the creation of a socialist society be impossible?... At this time Stalin's essay 'Trotskyism or Leninism?' appeared... Stalin refuted Trotsky's affirmations one by one. We could, he wrote, succeed in building socialism in our country... I agreed with Stalin's every word. He liberated me from all doubts. From then on, his essay was with me always.'

ATTACK AND COUNTER-ATTACK

In October 1924, Trotsky launched a public attack on Zinoviev and Kamenev in a book called *The Lessons of October*. He argued that they had betrayed the revolution, which he had led. Stalin, Zinoviev and Kamenev counter-attacked, accusing Trotsky of being 'anti-Leninist', and of breaking discipline by taking a political quarrel outside the party. Stalin even claimed that 'Comrade Trotsky did not, and could not, play any special part either in the party or in the October Revolution.'

TROTSKY DEFEATED

Thousands of young activists like Grigorenko (see box) took part in public demonstrations against Trotsky, in a well-organized campaign. In January 1925, Trotsky was removed from his post as head of the Red Army. He was no longer a serious rival for power.

With the defeat of Trotsky, Stalin had no further need of Zinoviev and Kamenev. He formed a new alliance, with Nikolai Bukharin. The economist was a strong defender of Lenin's New Economic Policy (NEP), allowing the peasants to sell their grain for profit. Bukharin saw the NEP as a way of gradually building a socialist society. The peasants' profits would be taxed, and the money raised would be used to build new industries. Meanwhile, through education, the peasants would be gradually won over to communist ideals. On 14 April 1925, *Pravda* published an article by Bukharin in which he addressed the peasantry: 'Enrich yourselves, develop your holdings. And don't worry that they may be taken away from you.'

ALLIES AND ENEMIES

To Zinoviev and Kamenev, this was the return of hated capitalism. They wanted to force the peasants on to large collective farms, transforming the countryside into a vast grain factory. The grain, sold abroad, could then be used to pay for rapid industrialization.

Stalin sided with Bukharin. In December 1925, when Zinoviev and Kamenev attacked Bukharin at the party congress, they were shouted down by Stalin's supporters.

Kamenev went to see Trotsky, and admitted that he had made a big mistake in backing Stalin. Kamenev said, 'You imagine that Stalin is preoccupied with how to reply to your arguments. Nothing of the kind. He is figuring out how to liquidate you without being punished.'

▲ A demonstration against Trotsky, whose cartoon appears alongside other enemies of the revolution.

19

TROTSKY'S FATE

Trotsky was exiled to Siberia in 1928 and, a year later, deported from the Soviet Union. He would spend the next decade moving from country to country, writing a stream of books and articles attacking Stalin, and continuing to call for world revolution. In 1936, Stalin ordered his secret police to hunt him down. One of Stalin's agents finally caught up with Trotsky in Mexico, in 1940, murdering him with an ice pick. At the time of his death, he was writing a biography of Stalin.

STALIN TAKES CONTROL

In desperation, Trotsky, Zinoviev and Kamenev buried their earlier differences and formed a 'united opposition' to Stalin. They had no hope of success. In 1927, all three were expelled from the Communist Party. Zinoviev and Kamenev were later readmitted, after publicly withdrawing their earlier views and denouncing Trotsky. Yet they never held high office again.

From 1926 until 1928, Stalin and Bukharin ruled the Soviet Union. Bukharin was the public face of the leadership, but he had no real power base without Stalin. As soon as Stalin decided not to follow Bukharin's policies, Bukharin's power evaporated.

Bukharin's policy of a free market for the peasants led to 1926 and 1927 being good years in the countryside. Yet this policy eventually ran into trouble, with a crisis in grain supply to the cities, in the winter of 1927–8. When the

▼ Trotsky in exile in Mexico, shortly before Stalin had him murdered.

▲ In 1930, Stalin stands beside former ally, Nikolai Bukharin, with whom he had fallen out.

government set prices too low, the peasants withheld their produce. Stalin convinced himself that it would have to be taken by force. In January 1928, Stalin's armed squads of policemen and party activists descended on the countryside. Stalin personally led the campaign in Siberia, where he saw for himself how unpopular his grain seizures were. This was the last time he visited a farm in his life.

SUCCESS AT A COST

The campaign was successful in that grain was seized and the cities were fed. Yet it cost the Communist Party the support that Bukharin's economic policies had gradually won from the peasants. The free market had given them an incentive to work. Now they had no reason to grow anything. Bukharin described Stalin's policy as a return to 'war communism, throat cutting', and believed that it could only lead to disaster.

AN UNPRINCIPLED INTRIGUER

On 11 July 1928, Bukharin visited Kamenev and voiced his despair at Stalin's new line. Kamenev took notes of the conversation to send to Zinoviev. Within a few months, Bukharin's description of Stalin had been smuggled abroad and published:

'Stalin's line is disastrous for the whole revolution... I have not spoken with Stalin for several weeks. He is an unprincipled intriguer, who subordinates everything to the preservation of his own power. He changes his theory according to whom he needs to get rid of... Our situation is desperate. If the country perishes, we perish. If the country survives, and Stalin changes his line in time, we perish anyway... What can we do in the face of an adversary of this sort?'

CHAPTER FOUR

Revolution From Above

THE RUSH TO MODERNIZE

By 1929, Stalin was undisputed ruler of the Soviet Union. Now that Zinoviev and Kamenev were no longer his rivals, Stalin decided to adopt their policies, of rapid industrialization, and collectivization of the land. The peasants were to be forced to give up their private holdings and work together on large collective farms. Stalin later called his new policy a 'revolution from above'.

In October 1928, Gosplan, the State Planning Commission, had created a 'Five Year Plan', setting modest targets for industrial development over five years. In April 1929, Stalin announced that these targets were to be dramatically raised. Coal and iron output would be doubled, while steel production would be tripled.

▼ Stalin watches over his Five Year Plan for industrialization.

FULL STEAM AHEAD

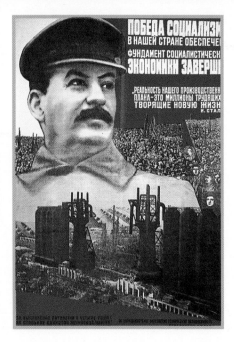

In November 1929, *Pravda* published Stalin's article, 'The Year of Great Change', in which he wrote:

'We are advancing full steam ahead along the path of industrialization – to socialism, leaving behind the age-long Russian backwardness. We are becoming a country of metal, a country of automobiles, a country of tractors. And when we have put the U.S.S.R. on an automobile, and the *muzhik* (peasant) on a tractor, let the esteemed capitalists, who boast so loudly of their "civilization", try to overtake us!'

THE ONE AND ONLY!

On 21 December 1929, Stalin used his fiftieth birthday celebrations to launch his own personality cult. The newspapers and the radio were filled with flattering messages of congratulation for the *vozhd* (boss), as Stalin was now called. His portrait appeared everywhere, beside Lenin. Over the years, praise for Stalin grew ever more exaggerated until he was called 'The Greatest Genius in History'. This sentiment, from the novelist Alexei Tolstoy, was typical:

'I want to howl, roar, shriek, bawl with rapture at the thought that we are living in the days of the most glorious, the one and only, incomparable, Stalin!'

Even Stalin joined in his chorus of praise. He wrote the following passage, which he

shamelessly inserted in his own official biography:
'Although he performed his task as leader of the party and the people with consummate skill and enjoyed the unreserved support of the entire Soviet people, Stalin never allowed his work to be marred by the slightest hint of vanity, conceit or self-adulation.'

There would be vast new industrial projects, including tractor factories, dams, and hydroelectric stations which would use water power to generate electricity. The whole nation would be put to work like an army, in the rush to modernize the Soviet Union.

The Five Year Plan was enthusiastically welcomed by young party activists, such as Petro Grigorenko, who later remembered, 'It was a time of great deeds… Stalin was able to keep discovering new challenges, and we looked to the beckoning horizons as if under a spell.'

▲ The different peoples of the Soviet Union gaze adoringly at Stalin, who had begun his own 'personality cult'.

КУЛАКИ САМЫЕ ЗВЕРСКИЕ, САМЫЕ ГРУБЫЕ, САМЫЕ ДИКИЕ, ЭКСПЛОАТАТОРЫ, НЕ РАЗ ВОССТАНАВЛИВАВШИЕ В ИСТОРИИ ДРУГИХ СТРАН ВЛАСТЬ ПОМЕЩИКОВ, ЦАРЕЙ, ПОПОВ. И КАПИТАЛИСТОВ.
ЛЕНИН.

ДОЛОЙ КУЛАКА ИЗ КОЛХОЗА

▲ This poster proclaims, 'Bash the kulak off the collective farm'. The fat 'kulak', or successful farmer, was said to be the main enemy of collective farming.

IT'S WAR

Victor Kravchenko was a young engineering student who took part in the campaign against the kulaks. Before they were sent to the countryside, Kravchenko and his fellow activists listened to a speech from a high-ranking communist, Comrade Hatayevich:

'... act like Bolsheviks worthy of Comrade Stalin. Beat the kulak agent down wherever he raises his head. It's war – it's them or us!... Don't be afraid of taking extreme measures... Comrade Stalin expects it of you. It's a life-and-death struggle.'

CLASS WAR IN THE COUNTRYSIDE

Soon after coming to power, the Bolsheviks had created two new types of farm: the *sovkhoz* (state-run farm), which operated like a factory, with wages paid to the peasants; and the *kolkhoz* (collectively-run farm), set up when peasants pooled their land, farming it as a co-operative. Only the poorest peasants could be persuaded to join these farms. In 1927, 99 per cent of the land was still farmed privately.

In launching his 'revolution from above', Stalin's aim was to destroy private farming. He believed that the way to do this was to start a new class war in the countryside. The enemy was the kulak (meaning 'fist'), an abusive name for a successful peasant farmer. Stalin announced that the kulaks had to be 'liquidated as a class' so that collective farming could be properly established. He said that the war would be fought on behalf of the 'poor and middle peasants', who were supposed to be eager to join collectives.

The war was fought by around 25,000 activists – factory workers and students – backed up by squads of armed policemen. They were ordered to seize the land and property of kulaks, and to convince the poor and middle peasants of the benefits of collective farming.

THE PEASANTS FLEE

The problem for the peasants was that the Communist Party provided no clear definition of what a kulak was. In practice, any peasants who resisted collectivization could be called kulaks, and have their possessions taken away from them. They were either driven from their homes and left to survive as best they could; or arrested and deported in cattle trucks to icy and remote parts of the Soviet Union.

At the same time, the Church, which had been the heart of peasant life, was attacked. Village churches and monasteries were stripped of their hangings, bells and icons (religious pictures), and converted into grain stores and stables.

Most peasants did not want to join collective farms. They showed their resistance by destroying crops and by slaughtering and eating their farm animals. Between 1929 and 1932, livestock numbers in the Soviet Union fell by a half. In the same period, nine million peasants fled the countryside, moving to the towns to look for work.

▼ Monasteries and churches were emptied of their valuables, in an organized Communist attack on religion.

LET THE GRAIN PERISH

Many peasants in collectives saw little reason to work. In 1930, Petro Grigorenko visited one farm during harvest time, where he was shocked by the attitude of the peasants:

'Arkhangelka, an enormous steppe [treeless plain] village of more than 2,000 farmhouses, was dead during the height of the harvest season... [Workers]... sat around or lay in the shade. When I tried to start conversations people replied slowly and with total indifference. If I told them that the grain was falling from wheat stalks and perishing they would reply, "Of course, it will perish."'

DEVASTATING LOSSES

By 1932, Stalin had managed to force over 60 per cent of the peasants on to collective farms. Yet what he could not do was make these farms deliver grain. By 'liquidating the kulaks', he had removed the most efficient farmers. The new collectives were run by party functionaries, who often knew little about farming. Just as devastating was the effect of the loss of the farm animals, which were needed to pull carts and ploughs, and to manure the soil.

In the autumn of 1932, there was a fall in farm production. Stalin decided that the peasants were deliberately concealing the grain. Remembering his own successful campaign of grain seizure, in 1928, he decided to reapply the same tactics. Once more, armed squads descended on the farms, taking away all the grain that they could find.

▼ Communist activists search for hidden grain.

FOR THEIR OWN GOOD

Lev Kopelev, who was a young activist, recalled his role in the 1932–3 grain seizures:

'I emptied out the old folks' storage chests, stopping my ears to the children's crying and the women's wails. For I was convinced that I was accomplishing the great and necessary transformation of the countryside; that in the days to come the people who lived there would be better off for it.'

FAMINE RETURNS

By the beginning of winter, there was another terrible famine, which only struck the countryside. While some five million peasants starved to death, the cities continued to be fed, and grain continued to be exported abroad. The famine was never mentioned in the papers, and Stalin denied its existence. In 1933, a party official reported to Stalin on the famine in the Ukraine. He replied, 'It seems that you are a good storyteller, you've made up such a fable about famine, thinking to frighten us, but it won't work.'

Some historians believe that this was a 'terror famine', deliberately planned by Stalin to crush the resistance of the peasantry. Others argue that Stalin did not intend, or even understand, the effect of his policies in the countryside.

▲ Victims of famine lie on a street in the Ukraine, in 1933.

▼ Stalin's wife and daughter.

A SUICIDE

In October 1932, Stalin's second wife, Nadezhda, whom he had married in 1919, was studying engineering at Moscow's Industrial Academy. Fellow students, who had been to the Ukraine, told her about the starvation in the villages, hoping that she would tell her husband. Deeply shocked, Nadezhda confronted Stalin. He refused to listen, and stopped his wife going to the academy. On 8 November 1932, she killed herself. Stalin is supposed to have said of her, 'She left me as an enemy!'

▲ The steel factories of Magnitogorsk, the show-piece of the Five Year Plans.

While the peasants starved in the countryside, Stalin's 'Five Year Plan' for industrialization was going ahead. Although it was called a plan, there was little real planning involved. Gosplan invented production quotas, or targets, which were then continually raised by Stalin. To push the workers harder, Stalin even announced that the Five Year Plan 'must be fulfilled in four years'. This became a famous slogan: '2+2=5'.

For Communists, this was a period of great optimism. In 1929, the US stock market crashed, leading to mass unemployment throughout the capitalist west. Meanwhile, the Soviet Union was able to put the whole nation to work. Communism seemed to be the way forward, and many Western engineers and workers emigrated to the Soviet Union to help build the new society.

THE IRON AND THE STEEL FRONT

US engineer John Scott described the building of the great steel-producing town at Magnitogorsk:

'Tens of thousands of people were enduring the most intense hardships in order to build blast furnaces, and many of them did it willingly... A quarter of a million souls... making the biggest steel *combinat* [factory complex] in Europe in the middle of the barren Ural steppe.'

The Five Year Plan was marked by inefficiency and waste. The factory workers were poorly trained peasants, who did not know how to look after their machines; these frequently broke down. Since quantity, not quality, was the main aim, many of the finished goods turned out to be useless.

WRECKERS

Rather than admit that his plan was at fault, Stalin blamed its many failures on organized sabotage. In a 1933 speech proclaiming the success of the Five Year Plan, Stalin warned that kulaks, former 'Whites', and other class enemies had infiltrated the factories:
'These 'have-beens' have crept into our plants and factories... and concealed themselves, donning the mask of 'workers' and 'peasants'... They are doing as much mischief as they can... They set fire to warehouses and break machines. They organize sabotage. They organize wrecking activities in the collective farms...

    A strong and powerful dictatorship of the proletariat – that is what we must have now in order to scatter the last remnants of the dying classes to the winds.'

For the workers, life was hard, with strict discipline, long hours, low wages, and poor food. They lived in makeshift huts and tents beside the huge factories they were building.

▼ Despite their hardships, many factory workers, like these youths, felt optimistic, certain that they were building a better society.

CHAPTER FIVE

The Great Terror

A SUSPICIOUS MURDER

On 1 December 1934, Sergei Mironovitch Kirov, the head of the Leningrad branch of the Communist Party, was shot dead outside his office. The killer was a disgruntled Communist called Leonid Nikolaev. After shooting Kirov, he fainted, and was found lying beside his victim.

Stalin reacted to the murder by rushing through an emergency law, ending party members' protection from the death penalty. One of the first to be executed, after a hurried trial, was Nikolaev.

Stalin would use Kirov's death as an excuse to launch a campaign of terror against his opponents in the Communist Party. It would allow him to kill almost all the leaders from the revolutionary period, and many thousands of ordinary people.

DID STALIN KILL KIROV?

Alexander Orlov was an agent of the NKVD (secret police) who fled to the West. In 1954, he published a sensational book called *The Secret History of Stalin's Crimes*.

Based on NKVD gossip, Orlov claimed that Stalin had ordered Kirov's murder. Stalin's motive was supposed to be jealousy at Kirov's popularity in the party, and the need for a pretext for terror. According to Orlov, the Leningrad NKVD encouraged and trained the assassin, who was known to be unbalanced, and then deliberately failed to protect Kirov.

Nikita Khrushchev, who succeeded Stalin as Soviet leader, said that many suspicious circumstances surrounded the killing. Before the murder, Kirov's bodyguard, Borisov, had twice arrested Nikolaev, whom he caught with his revolver, only to see him released by the secret police. At the time of Kirov's murder at the hands of Nikolaev, Borisov was detained outside the building by secret policemen. The following day, Borisov was murdered by the NKVD, who were bringing him in for questioning.

The evidence does seem to point to NKVD involvement in Kirov's death. Yet the case against Stalin remains unproven. The only certainty is that he was the one person who benefited from the killing.

30

'THE KIROV FLOOD'

In the weeks following the murder, there were thousands of arrests of 'enemies of the people'. Between 1934 and 1935, the number of those sent to prisons and labour camps more than tripled, rising from 59,451 to 185,846. Prison inmates called these newcomers 'the Kirov flood'.

The first to be arrested were followers of Zinoviev, who still had many supporters in Leningrad from his time as party chief there. Shortly after Kirov's killing, Elkin Leikin visited his friend Zinoviev in his Moscow apartment. Leikin found Zinoviev gazing out of the window at a group of angry demonstrators, who were demanding death for the murderers of Kirov. 'They will pin this on us,' said Zinoviev, 'This is the beginning of a great tragedy.'

A CLIMATE OF FEAR

A Czech journalist, J. Bernard Hutton, described the atmosphere following the murder of Kirov:

'The "Black Ravens" [police vans] were on the move day and night as especially selected NKVD officers arrested suspects in factories, offices... Always in the early hours of the morning. I would hear their nailed jackboots stamping in the corridors, the doors banging, their shouting and cursing. Nobody knew whose turn would come next. It went on for weeks and weeks.'

◄ Stalin helps carry the ashes of the murdered Kirov, whose face looks down from a huge poster.

31

STALIN'S PIPE

A Russian joke pointed out the ease with which the NKVD was able to make people confess to imaginary crimes:

Stalin loses his pipe and asks the NKVD to find it. Two hours later, he finds it in his boot, and telephones the NKVD to ask what progress they are making. They tell him that ten men have been arrested.

'I've found my pipe, so release them at once.'

'But seven have confessed already.'

THE TERROR ESCALATES

Stalin's terror developed its own momentum. Like everyone else in the Soviet Union, the NKVD had quotas to meet. They had set numbers of 'enemies of the people' to find. Every arrested person was forced to sign confessions, naming people who had acted with them, who were then arrested in turn. Anyone with a grievance against anyone else could get rid of them by denouncing them to the NKVD. No evidence was needed to arrest anyone. Failure to act on an accusation would be seen as 'lack of vigilance' by the secret police.

Since everyone was innocent, nobody felt safe from arrest. The terror was even turned against the secret

▼ NKVD chief Nikolai Ezhov is shown crushing enemies of the people, including Trotsky, in his iron glove.

UNCLE JOE

In July 1936, Stalin went for a walk in the woods with his nephew, Budu Svanidze, who later recorded his uncle's conversation:

'Getting rid of the vermin by themselves would be easy. Unfortunately, there are too many comrades [Communists] who support them because they don't want to understand the necessity for combat and destruction. So we have to get rid of them too… We can't help it. As the wisdom of the people puts it, we must hew [cut] to the line, let the chips fall where they may.'

police itself. In 1936, Stalin complained that it had been 'four years late' in unmasking enemies. He sacked the NKVD chief, Genrikh Yagoda, and later had him shot. Yagoda's replacement, Nikolai Ezhov, then executed 3,000 top NKVD officers.

STALIN'S REASONS

Every victim of the terror wondered about the purpose behind it. The words 'why?' and 'what for?' were scratched on countless prison cell walls. In the camps, prisoners argued and came up with various theories. One idea was that Stalin wanted to get rid of all the old Bolsheviks, those who knew the truth about his undistinguished role in the revolution. Some said that fascist agents had wormed their way into the NKVD. A few even thought that the whole terrible experience was a kind of test, to find out if they were true believers in communism; if they passed the test, they would be released.

Historians still argue about the real causes. Some argue that the terror was carefully planned by Stalin, to remove potential opposition within the party, and to frighten the population, making it easier to rule. Others see it as another chaotic process, like the collectivization campaign, in which Stalin was unable to control the forces he had unleashed.

STALIN'S OPPONENTS ON TRIAL

In 1936, Stalin organized the first of three 'show trials' of his former opponents. The defendants, against whom the charges were brought, were Zinoviev, Kamenev and

▶ The aim of the show trials was to demonstrate that Stalin's political opponents were part of a conspiracy, led by Trotsky, in the pay of Nazi Germany. This cartoon shows Trotsky as a terrorist carrying a bomb and standing on a Nazi swastika.

THE MAD DOGS MUST BE SHOT!

Andrei Vyshinsky, prosecutor at the show trial, summed up:

'With great and peerless love the toilers [workers] of the whole world speak the name of Joseph Vissarionovich Stalin, the name of that great teacher and leader... From their gloomy underworld, Trotsky, Zinoviev and Kamenev have therefore sent this despicable call: thrust him aside, kill him!... Our whole people has risen to its feet since these ghastly crimes have become known... I demand that the mad dogs be shot!'

fourteen associates. They publicly confessed that they had been part of a huge conspiracy, led by Trotsky, to destroy the Soviet Union with the help of foreign powers. They had organized wrecking (see page 29), had murdered Kirov, and had tried to kill Stalin.

Various methods were used to get the accused to confess. Kamenev and Zinoviev were kept in heated cells, at the height of summer, and worn down by continuous questioning. They were told that their families would be killed if they did not co-operate. The interrogators also appealed to their loyalty to the party, which was said to need this last service of them. The 1930s had seen a new threat to the Soviet Union with the coming to power of the Nazi Party in Germany. Kamenev and Zinoviev were told that their confessions would help unite the country behind the Soviet government. They eventually agreed to co-operate when Stalin promised to spare their lives.

At his trial, in August 1936, Zinoviev told a shocked Soviet public, 'I am guilty of having been the organizer, second only to Trotsky, of that bloc whose chosen task was the killing of Stalin… I was the principle organizer of Kirov's assassination.'

Stalin broke his word to the defendants, who were shot in the cellars of the Lubyanka, the Moscow secret police headquarters, just 24 hours after the trial.

▲ In factories, workers listened to radio broadcasts of the trials, and then voted to support the death penalties given to the accused.

OUR HEADS IN HIS MOUTH

Shortly before the Zinoviev trial, Stalin had allowed Bukharin to go to Paris, where he visited two old friends, Fyodor and Lydia Dan. Bukharin told them that Stalin was 'a small spiteful man, no, not a man, a devil'. When they asked him why he remained loyal to him, Bukharin replied:

'You give your trust not to him, but to the man the party trusts, so that it has come about that he is as it were the symbol of the party... the people trust him – our fault perhaps, but that is how it turned out, and that is why we are all putting our heads in his mouth, knowing that he will probably eat us up. He knows this quite well and is just biding his time.'

Bukharin could not imagine life outside the Communist Party. He returned to the Soviet Union, where he would face his own show trial and execution in 1938.

WESTERN REACTION TO THE SHOW TRIALS

Western observers were baffled by Stalin's show trials. The British diplomat Fitzroy Maclean, who watched the trial of Bukharin in 1938, wrote:

'If what we had heard in court was the literal truth, if ever since the Revolution the highest offices of State had been held by a band of traitors, spies, murderers and wreckers... how was it that such a galaxy of talent, with such opportunities, had obtained so small a measure of success?'

Maclean could not understand why the accused seemed so eager to confess, and why they made no attempt to defend themselves, or even to criticize the Soviet regime they were supposed to have wanted to overthrow. The idea that the charges were false was just as baffling, as Maclean's colleague, Viscount Chilston explained:

'If... the charges are entirely or largely false, then power in this country must be wielded by maniacs, who in order to still their own insane suspicions and satisfy their mad lust for power, are murdering all those who might conceivably thwart their designs...'

HISTORY REWRITTEN

As well as Western observers, many Soviet citizens also found the trials hard to understand. However, it was impossible for them to voice any doubts openly, for fear of being denounced to the NKVD. The only people who could talk freely were those already in prison. Stalin had set about creating what historians call a 'totalitarian' society (based on a single dictatorial party), where all sources of information were strictly controlled, and total loyalty was demanded of every citizen.

Stalin even controlled people's knowledge of the past. History books were rewritten, wiping out Trotsky's contribution to the revolution and civil war. Photographs of the revolutionary leadership were also retouched, removing Trotsky, Kamenev and Zinoviev. The English novelist George Orwell described this process in his novel, *1984*: 'The past, starting from yesterday, has actually been abolished... History has stopped. Nothing exists except an endless present in which the party is always right.'

◀ ▲ Stalin had many photographs altered, to remove those with whom he had quarrelled from the historical record. It was as if such people had never existed.

SAFETY FIRST

US journalist Louis Fischer described life in the Soviet Union in the late 1930s: 'Everybody played safety first. Lying, hypocrisy... violence towards one's deepest conviction, and disloyalty to friends were a small price to pay for keeping out of prison. To divert suspicion from yourself, you accuse the other fellow... When Stalin's name was mentioned, you applauded and you did not stop even though it might go on for ten minutes.'

THE RED ARMY PURGED

On 11 June 1937, the Soviet press announced that the Red Army's eight most senior generals had been arrested, and had confessed to treachery on behalf of Germany and Japan. Confessions were beaten out of the generals by the NKVD. The signed confession of the senior general, Marshal Mikhail Tukhachevsky, still exists in the Russian archives. The paper is dotted with brown stains which have been analysed, and found to be human blood.

The generals were all shot on 12 June. The NKVD was then turned on the lower ranks of the Red Army. In the following purge, 9,941 officers were arrested and 23,434 were dismissed. This was a devastating blow to the army's effectiveness. It had lost its best and most experienced commanders, the generation that had fought and won the civil war.

▼ Marshals Tukhachevsky (right) and Yegorov (left) were both shot on Stalin's orders. The Red Army was now run by men like Marshal Voroshilov (centre) who was loyal to Stalin, but incompetent.

OUT OF CONTROL

The terror became more intense after the 'army plot'. Before 1937, most victims had been people who had belonged to former opposition groups, such as supporters

THE GREAT TERROR ★

of Zinoviev and Bukharin. Now, for the first time, loyal supporters of Stalin were arrested. In the second half of 1937, nearly all the regional party secretaries were shot. The terror also spread beyond the Communist Party to the wider population, in a blind mass panic of arrests and executions.

By late 1938, Stalin realized that the terror had spun out of control, undermining the Communist Party's ability to function and rule the country. He called a halt to the mass arrests, placing the blame on Nikolai Ezhov, the NKVD chief. Ezhov, accused of being a Polish spy, was shot in 1940. Stalin put the blame on Ezhov for the whole terror, which was popularly known as the Ezhovshchina (Ezhov times).

A REAL CONSPIRACY

Although there is no evidence that the generals had plotted against Stalin, he acted as if he really believed in their guilt. NKVD agent Alexander Orlov wrote: 'That was a real conspiracy! That could be seen from the panic which spread there on the top: all passes to the Kremlin were suddenly declared invalid. Our [NKVD] troops were held in a state of alarm...

The whole Soviet government hung by a thread.'

This was confirmed by Stalin's associate, Viacheslav Molotov, when he was interviewed in the 1970s. Molotov said that while mistakes had been made during the terror, Tukhachevsky was truly guilty of treason. He said, 'He was hurrying with a coup... we even knew the date of the coup.'

Stalin may have been the victim of a clever plot by the German secret police. In order to destroy Tukhachevsky and cripple the Red Army, the Germans had forged letters between the Marshal Tukhachevsky and the senior German generals. In May, these letters were 'leaked' to the Soviet Ambassador to Czechoslovakia, who immediately forwarded them to Stalin.

◀ Under Ezhov's successor, Lavrenti Beria, the number of NKVD executions fell from 328,618 in 1938, to 2,552 in 1939.

A MODEL PRISON

In the 1930s, Stalin was able to keep secret from the West the terrible conditions of life in Soviet prisons and labour camps (see page 41). Foreign visitors to the Soviet Union were fooled by being shown a specially built 'model prison' at Bolshevo, just outside Moscow. This was described by the British writers Sidney and Beatrice Webb:

'It is situated on the pleasant country estate of an expropriated millionaire... where it combines manufacturing production with agriculture. It has no walls or locked gates interfering with the inmates' freedom to leave... [They are] set to work at piece-work wages, to be spent freely at the various departments of the prison shop; allowed to smoke and to talk, to enjoy music and the theatre... Many refuse to leave on the expiration [end] of their sentences there.'

THE GULAGS

▼ Prisoners at work, digging the Baltic–White Sea canal by hand.

Stalin was to publicize another use of prisoners, in the construction of the 220km-long Baltic-White Sea canal, built in 1930-3. This was dug by 250,000 prisoners using only shovels and picks. The project was praised as a way

Stalin with Kirov and Voroshilov, at the grand opening of the canal, which later proved to be useless.

of re-educating offenders through useful work. Nobody was told that most of the prisoners were innocent of any crime; nor that over half of them died building the canal; nor that when it was completed it turned out to be useless. The canal was too shallow for ships.

Labour camps sprang up across the Soviet Union in the 1930s, run by a branch of the NKVD called GULAG (Chief Administration of Corrective Labour Camps). These were often in remote regions, such as Siberia and the Arctic Circle, which were rich in natural resources, such as gold. Since it was impossible to attract people to work in such places, the idea of using forced labour seemed the obvious solution.

The prisoners were underfed, and were punished for not working hard enough by having their rations further cut. The result was a vicious circle, in which prisoners who grew too weak to work were starved to death. There were always plenty of new prisoners to take their place.

CAMPS IN KOLYMA

The most notorious camps were those at Kolyma in eastern Siberia, where gold was mined. Every tonne of gold was said to have cost the lives of 1,000 prisoners. Varlam Shalamov, who was imprisoned there, explained Kolyma's high death rate:

'In the camp, it took twenty to thirty days to turn a healthy man into a wreck. Working in the camp mine sixteen hours a day, without any days off, with systematic starvation, ragged clothes, sleeping in a torn tent at 60 below zero, did the job. Beatings by the foremen, by the thieves, by the guards, speeded up the process... The gold mine steadily cast its waste products into the hospitals... and into common graves.'

CHAPTER SIX

Stalin's Foreign Policy

SIEGE MENTALITY

From the time he came to power, Stalin stressed the threat from enemies abroad. He justified the need for rapid industrialization and a strong dictatorship because of 'capitalist encirclement'. In other words the Soviet Union was like a fortress, besieged by hostile capitalist nations, who would attack at the slightest sign of weakness. Stalin used this threat to create a permanent state of emergency.

▶ Adolf Hitler, the German dictator, inspects a Nazi parade in 1934. Hitler was to prove Stalin's deadliest foe.

In fact, until the mid 1930s, there was never a real danger of a foreign invasion. Although the capitalist nations, such as Britain and France, hated communism, after the horrors of the First World War, they were desperate to keep the peace.

THE RISE OF THE NAZI PARTY

Everything changed in 1933, when Adolf Hitler's Nazi Party came to power in Germany. Hitler was actually helped to power by Stalin, who wrongly thought that Germany's moderate Social Democrats, who competed with the German Communist Party for working-class support, were his real enemies. Through his control of the Comintern (see page 14) Stalin prevented the German Communists forming an alliance with the Social Democrats, which might have stopped the Nazis. Stalin underestimated Hitler, thinking that he would be unable to hold on to power.

After becoming chancellor of Germany, Hitler showed decisiveness and brutality against his opponents. His first victims were thousands of German Communists, who were arrested in February 1934. Stalin soon realized that he had made a mistake. Hitler wanted to unite the German nation, and make it great by conquering other nations. He would prove to be the most dangerous enemy Stalin ever faced.

HITLER AND STALIN

Hitler and Stalin were alike in many ways. Each man was a loner. Each saw life as an endless struggle against enemies. They also shared the aim of creating a totalitarian system (see page 36), with complete control over the lives and even the thoughts of their citizens.

The key difference was in their set of beliefs. While communism was an international movement, based on the struggle between classes, Nazism was nationalistic, and based on race. Hitler believed that the German race was superior to other 'lesser' races, and had the right to rule them. His greatest hatred was for the Jews, partly because they were an international race. Since many leading Communists, including Marx and Trotsky, were Jewish, Hitler believed that communism was a Jewish conspiracy. In fact, Stalin also hated Jews, making many anti-Jewish comments in private conversation; in public he took care to hide this prejudice.

If Stalin had read Hitler's 1926 autobiography, *Mein Kampf (My Struggle)*, he might have been less willing to help him take power. Here, Hitler announced that his aim was 'to secure for the German people the land and soil to which they are entitled... If we speak of soil in Europe today, we can primarily have in mind only Russia... The giant empire in the East is ripe for collapse.'

▲ A communist poster from the Spanish Civil War. Although Stalin supported the republican side, he spent as much time hunting down Trotskyists as he did fighting Franco.

SPANISH CIVIL WAR

In the summer of 1936, General Francisco Franco led a military uprising in Spain, to overthrow the democratically elected republic. Hitler, and the Italian fascist dictator, Mussolini, backed Franco in the civil war, supplying him with tanks, planes and troops. The republican side was supported only by the Soviet Union, which gave limited military support.

Britain and France's refusal to help the Spanish republic led Stalin to doubt whether they had the will to resist Hitler. This was a major blow to collective security (working together for peace).

OPPOSING FASCISM

From 1934, Stalin's foreign policy was aimed at forming defensive alliances against Nazi Germany. In 1935, he called for a 'popular front', or collaboration amongst all the enemies of fascism. To make this new policy work, Stalin had to reassure the Western democracies, France and Britain, that communism was not a threat. In 1936, US journalist Roy Howard asked Stalin, 'Has the Soviet Union abandoned its plans to carry out world revolution?' Stalin replied, 'We never had any such intentions.'

Having spent years denouncing the League of Nations, set up by the Western powers after the First World War, Stalin joined the League in 1936. At League meetings, the Soviets called for disarmament (reduction of weapons), collective security and resistance to aggression. The same year, Stalin signed a military treaty with France, in which each nation promised to aid the other if attacked.

AN END TO COLLECTIVE SECURITY

In 1938, British Prime Minister Chamberlain and French Premier Daladier signed an agreement with Hitler at Munich. It allowed Hitler to seize part of neighbouring Czechoslovakia in return for a promise that he would make no more demands. Stalin, furious that he had not even been consulted, now knew that collective security was dead.

In March 1939, Hitler invaded the rest of Czechoslovakia, breaking the promises he had made at Munich. The following month Chamberlain gave a military guarantee to protect Poland, Hitler's next target.

What Chamberlain did not realize was that Stalin had begun secret negotiations with Hitler, which resulted in a non-aggression pact, signed in August 1939. This gave Hitler a free hand to attack Poland, and made war between Germany and the democracies of France and Britain inevitable.

▼ A smiling Stalin stands beside Ribbentrop, the German foreign minister, while his own minister, Molotov, signs the pact with Nazi Germany.

STALIN'S REASONS

Stalin's pact with Hitler was one of the greatest about-faces in history. On 19 August 1939, Stalin told the rest of the Politburo why he had decided to enter into the pact:

'If Germany is victorious, she will emerge from the war too exhausted to be able to start a military conflict with the USSR, at least for a decade... We must do everything possible to ensure that this war lasts as long as possible to ensure the exhaustion of both parties.'

CHAPTER SEVEN

The Great Patriotic War

STALIN'S MISCALCULATION

▼ A German poster promising to attack the Soviet Union with a knock-out blow. The cross with Churchill's name on was an attempt to reassure people that Britain had lost the war. In fact, Germany would now be fighting on two fronts.

Stalin took it for granted that the new war would be a repeat of the First World War, in which rival armies fought to a standstill, facing each other from lines of trenches. Until the Germans conquered part of Poland in September 1939 Stalin did not discover that they had invented a new way of fighting, called 'blitzkrieg' (lightning war), using speed and surprise to paralyse and overwhelm enemy forces. He was also to underestimate the power of blitzkrieg to conquer France. The only Soviet general who understood blitzkrieg was Marshal Tukhachevsky, but Stalin had had him shot.

Using blitzkrieg, it took the *Wehrmacht* (German army) less than a month to defeat the Poles. Once the real fighting was over, the Red Army marched into eastern Poland, which Hitler had granted to Stalin in a secret section of the Nazi–Soviet Pact.

While Stalin was impressed by the German victory over Poland, he still expected a long war in the west. He was sure that France, with the largest army in Europe, would be a match for Hitler. So it was with growing horror that he watched the *Wehrmacht* win one easy victory after another. By May 1940, the *Wehrmacht* had conquered Denmark, Norway, Belgium and France, and driven the British army into the sea at Dunkirk.

W CHURCHILL

Europas Sieg dein wohlstand

A DISASTROUS WAR

In November 1939, Stalin had begun his own war against Finland, a tiny country with a small army. This war was a disaster for the Red Army, which lost 126,000 men – six times higher than Finnish losses. This confirmed the weakness of the Red Army, following Stalin's execution of all his best generals. Meanwhile the *Wehrmacht* seemed invincible.

Stalin's Finnish disaster convinced Hitler that the Soviet Union could be conquered just as swiftly as France. He said to his generals, 'We have only to kick in the door and the whole rotten structure will come crashing down.'

WARNINGS DISCOUNTED

By the summer of 1941, Stalin had received warnings from 76 different sources that Hitler was planning to attack the Soviet Union. Stalin ignored them all, believing that the British were sending him false information, aimed at dragging him into the war.

Right up until the day Germany invaded, Stalin continued to supply Hitler with oil and other raw materials, under the terms of the Nazi–Soviet pact. Even when it was clear that German troops were massing on the Soviet borders, Stalin refused to mobilize the Red Army. He did not want to do anything which might provoke a German attack. Stalin, who had never trusted anyone in his life before, continued to act as if he trusted Hitler.

'HITLER WILL NOT ATTACK...'

On 21 June 1941, on the eve of the German invasion, police chief Lavrenti Beria wrote to Stalin:

'Our ambassador in Berlin, Dekanozov... is bombarding me with 'disinformation' that Hitler is allegedly preparing to attack the Soviet Union. He stated that this 'attack' will begin tomorrow... But I and my people, Joseph Vissarionovich, firmly remember your wise prognosis: Hitler will not attack us in 1941!'

ADVANCE AND RETREAT

In the first months of the war, the German advance was unstoppable. The *Wehrmacht* advanced deep into Soviet territory, overwhelming all opposition. In the towns of the Ukraine, Germans were even welcomed as liberators.

Yet Hitler was not prepared for the immense size of the country he had invaded, nor for its primitive roads. With the autumn rains, the roads turned to rivers of mud, slowing the *Wehrmacht's* advance. This came to a complete halt with the coming of the

▲ The frozen bodies of German soldiers, unprepared for the Russian winter.

STALIN OFFERS TO RESIGN

A week after the German invasion began, Stalin retired to his house outside Moscow, where he hinted that he might resign. This is how Nikolai Bulganin remembered Stalin's conversation with the Politburo:

'He looked gloomy. He said... *"Maybe some among you wouldn't mind putting all the blame on me."*

Molotov: *"I tell you here and now that if some idiot tried to turn me against you, I'd see him damned. We are asking you to come back to work... "*

"Yes, but think about it: can I live up to people's hopes any more? Can I lead the country to final victory? There may be more deserving candidates."

Voroshilov: *"I believe that I shall be voicing the unanimous opinion: there is none more worthy."* There was an immediate chorus of "Right!"'

Stalin's offer to resign may have been genuine, or he may have said this to test the loyalty of his colleagues. Whatever his reason, by 1 July, Stalin was back at the Kremlin (the government offices), in charge of the war effort.

coldest winter in living memory. The oil in the tanks froze, and thousands of German soldiers, still wearing their summer uniforms, died of frostbite.

In the middle of this bitter winter, Stalin launched a counter-attack, using Siberian troops who were trained to fight in winter conditions. For the first time in the Second World War, the Germans were forced into a retreat.

WAR EFFORT

ПОДВИГАМЪ ДОБЛЕСТИ СЛАВА, ЧЕСТЬ, ПАМЯТЬ.

ПУСТЬ ВДОХНОВЛЯЕТ ВАС В ЭТОЙ ВОЙНЕ МУЖЕСТВЕННЫЙ ОБРАЗ НАШИХ ВЕЛИКИХ ПРЕДКОВ!

И. СТАЛИН

The Soviet economy was much better suited to fighting an all-out war than the German economy. Central control made it possible for the Soviets to move entire industries east, out of reach of the German guns, and then convert the factories to making tanks and planes. Throughout the 1930s, Stalin had run the country as if it were at war, mobilizing the entire nation in his Five Year Plans, and demanding endless sacrifices. This made it easier for the Soviet people to accept the sacrifices of war.

Hitler had never asked the German people to accept sacrifices, for his conquests had come so easily. Instead of switching to an all-out war effort, German factories continued to produce luxury goods throughout the war. Hitler could not even bring himself to order German women to work in war factories, thinking that a woman's place was in the home, raising children. In contrast, Soviet women fought and died on the front lines, beside the men.

▲ Stalin's wartime posters stressed traditional Russian patriotism rather than communism. Here Soviet soldiers are watched over by Kutuzov, the heroic general who defeated an earlier invasion by Napoleon Bonaparte.

▲ This painting shows Stalin as Commander-in-Chief at the battle front, a place he never visited.

STALIN'S MILITARY STRATEGIES

At first, Stalin made many mistakes as Commander-in-Chief of the army. In 1942, he ordered the Red Army to go on the offensive (attack) on all fronts, before it had the proper resources. When the offensive failed with great losses, Stalin learned from his mistake. Increasingly, he allowed the generals to make the tactical decisions, while running the war as a manager. He made sure that his generals were provided with the troops and armaments they needed to fight the Germans.

In contrast, Hitler, who also saw himself as a great military strategist, learned nothing from his mistakes and refused to take advice from his generals. Hitler was obsessed with the idea that the *Wehrmacht* should not withdraw a single inch. This attitude was responsible for the *Wehrmacht's* defeat at the Battle of Stalingrad in February 1943, when the entire German Sixth Army was captured.

HEROIC LEADER OR FRIGHTENED RABBIT?

Nikita Khrushchev was the Politburo's representative at the front. In his memoirs, he described the Stalin of early 1942, now Commander-in-Chief of the Red Army:

'He had pulled himself together, straightened up, and was acting like a real soldier. He had also begun to think of himself as a great military strategist, which made it harder then ever to argue with him. He exhibited all the strong-willed determination of a heroic leader. But I knew what sort of a hero he was. I'd seen him when he had been paralysed by his fear of Hitler, like a rabbit in front of a boa constrictor.'

STALIN THE DIPLOMAT

The war forced Stalin to learn another new role, as a diplomat. For the first time, he had to negotiate face-to-face with other heads of state. British Prime Minister Churchill and US President Roosevelt met Stalin at Tehran in November 1943, to discuss the conduct of the war and the post-war settlement. One of the important issues under discussion was the future of Poland. The difficulty was that while Britain had gone to war to protect Poland's independence, Stalin on the other hand was determined to hold on to as much of Poland as he could conquer.

Stalin was a brilliant diplomat, able to manipulate Roosevelt with ease. Churchill distrusted Stalin, but also felt guilty that the Soviets were doing most of the fighting, and knew that there was little he could do to protect Poland. At Tehran, the Western leaders agreed to let Stalin have a large part of Poland.

ROOSEVELT'S HUNCH

William Bullitt, former US ambassador to the Soviet Union, warned President Roosevelt that Stalin would try to seize as much territory as possible following the war. The president replied:
'I just have a hunch that Stalin is not that kind of man... I think if I give him everything I possibly can and ask for nothing in return... he won't try to annex anything and will work with me for a world of democracy and peace... It's my responsibility... and I'm going to play my hunch.'

▼ Stalin, Roosevelt and Churchill meet at Tehran in Iran, in 1943.

STALIN'S SON

Among the war's victims was Stalin's eldest son, Yakov, who died in a German prison camp. The Nazis had offered to exchange him for Marshal Paulus, captured at Stalingrad, but Stalin refused. Ashamed that his son had allowed himself to be taken prisoner, Stalin told a foreign journalist that there was no such thing as a Russian prisoner of war, only a Russian traitor.

BREAKING A PROMISE

By 1943, it was only a matter of time before Germany's final defeat. The Western allies and the Red Army now raced each other to liberate as much Nazi-held territory as possible.

The 'Big Three' held their second meeting at Yalta, in February 1945. At Yalta, the three leaders publicly declared that they would allow free elections in the countries they had liberated after the war. Stalin had no intention of keeping this promise, which he saw as one made solely for the public. He knew that the USA and Britain would seek to influence the type of governments they set up post-war, in countries such as Italy and Greece, and thought that he had the right to act in the same way.

When it became clear that Stalin would not allow a free election in Poland, now occupied by the Red Army, Roosevelt was shocked. 'We can't do business with Stalin,' he said privately, 'He has broken every one of the promises he made at Yalta.'

In May 1945, the Red Army captured Berlin, winning the war against Germany. This was Stalin's greatest triumph. He felt that it proved he had been right to follow his policies of the 1930s. Rapid industrialization had made the victory possible, and the terror had removed any 'enemies within', who might have threatened the unity of the nation.

THE BIRTH OF A SUPERPOWER

After the war, Stalin installed Communist governments throughout Central and Eastern Europe. None of

▼ A victorious Red Army soldier in Berlin with a souvenir to bring home, a bust of Adolf Hitler.

The Soviet Union and Eastern Europe, 1945 - 1948

North Sea

SWEDEN

FINLAND

NORWAY

Vyborg

Tallin (Reval)

Leningrad

ESTONIA

Baltic Sea

Riga

LATVIA

SOVIET UNION (Russia)

DENMARK

LITHUANIA

Königsberg

Vilna

Minsk

Stettin

East Prussia

Berlin

Warsaw

GERMANY

Silesia

POLAND

Bonn

Dresden

Prague Cracow

Lvov

Galicia

CZECHOSLOVAKIA

FRANCE

Munich

Vienna

AUSTRIA

Budapest

Bessarabia

Kishinev

SWITZERLAND

HUNGARY

ROMANIA

Trieste

ITALY

Belgrade

Bucharest

YUGOSLAVIA

BULGARIA

Black Sea

Adriatic Sea

ALBANIA

Sofia

Tirana

Aegean Sea

TURKEY

Caspian Sea

Mediterranean Sea

GREECE

0   1000km

0   600m

Key

Territory seized by Russia 1939-1940 and reincorporated in Russia in 1945

Territory seized by Russia in 1945

States freed by the Soviet army and in which Communist regimes came to power between 1945 and 1948

Russian occupation zones

British, French and American occupation zones

The 'Iron Curtain' in 1948

◀ Victory over Germany allowed Stalin to set up Communist governments across central Europe.

these countries had large communist parties, and the new governments depended on the threat of the Red Army to stay in power. The only Communist Party with any real support from the people was Josip Broz Tito's in Yugoslavia. Tito, who refused to take orders from the Soviet Union, replaced Trotsky in Stalin's mind as his greatest enemy.

The Soviet Union had become a superpower, yet the country's industries and collective farms were in ruins. Twenty-seven million Soviet citizens had lost their lives. Although the Soviets appeared strong, they felt weak in relation to the USA and threatened by the flood of US aid, used to support anti-communist governments in West Germany, Italy, Greece, Turkey and Japan. Mutual mistrust and misunderstandings soon resulted in a 'Cold War' between the former allies.

WE SHALL RECOVER

Milovan Djilas, a leading Yugoslav communist, recorded these words of Stalin in 1944:
'This war is not as in the past; whoever occupies a territory also imposes on it his own social system. Everyone imposes his own system as far as his army has power to do so. It cannot be otherwise... The war will soon be over. We shall recover in fifteen or twenty years, and then we'll have another go at it.'

CHAPTER EIGHT

Last Years

FURTHER REPRESSION

After the terrible sacrifices of the war, most Soviet citizens hoped that life would grow easier in peacetime. Instead, Stalin's dictatorship became even more repressive. In these years, the prison camp population doubled, from the wartime figure of 2.3 million, to 5 million by 1953. The numbers were swelled by Red Army soldiers and prisoners of war returning from the West – Stalin distrusted anybody who had been abroad. In 1949–50, he launched a new terror in Leningrad, where hundreds of party officials were arrested, tortured and shot. For the first time, Stalin also openly showed his anti-Semitism, having many prominent Soviet Jews arrested.

Stalin's suspiciousness increased until he came to think that his closest colleagues, Molotov, Voroshilov and Beria, were spies in the pay of foreign powers. Luckily for them, the boss's once famous memory was failing; increasingly senile, he began to forget even the names of the Politburo. In 1951, Nikita Khrushchev overheard Stalin saying to himself, 'I'm finished. I trust no one, not even myself.'

DEATH OF A DICTATOR

On 1 March 1953, Stalin did not come out of his bedroom as usual. For a whole day, his servants were too scared to open the door to his room. At 10pm, a bodyguard finally entered, finding Stalin unconscious on the floor. When

WHY ARE WE WEEPING?

Harrison Salisbury, US journalist, described the scenes in Moscow on the announcement of Stalin's death:
'I saw women crying in the streets of Moscow although the man they were crying for may very well have murdered their husband, or sent relatives to a concentration camp... A more common reaction was, "What's coming next? Will it be something worse?" As it might well be.'

Even in Siberia, people wept. Olga Infland, who had spent ten years as a labour camp inmate, recalled her own reaction:
'When Stalin died, there was a meeting, speeches were made, and we cried. Really, we were crying. Can you imagine? When we left the meeting, I said to my friend, "Why are we weeping?"'

the Politburo was summoned, Beria said to the bodyguard, 'What do you mean by starting a panic? The boss is obviously sleeping peacefully. Let's go.'

It was only the following day, thirteen hours after Stalin had been discovered, that doctors were finally called. They found that, like Lenin, he had suffered a massive stroke. He lingered on, unable to speak, until he died on 5 March.

The delay in seeking medical attention for the unconscious Stalin suggests that his colleagues were not eager for him to recover. He may even have been murdered. Beria, in particular, had good reasons for wanting to see Stalin dead – he had lost Stalin's trust, and knew that it was only a matter of time before he was arrested, like the two secret police chiefs before him. In an interview many years later, Molotov claimed that Beria had boasted, 'I took him out.'

◀ Russians in Moscow weep on hearing the news of Stalin's death. He had dominated their lives for so long that many found it hard to believe that he had gone.

CHAPTER NINE

Stalin's Heirs

THE STRUGGLE FOR POWER

While Stalin lay in state so that the public could see his body, the mourners standing beside his coffin were already involved in a power struggle. At first, Beria, with his control of the secret police (see page 39), seemed to be the victor, dominating the new government. Yet Beria underestimated the cunning of Nikita Khrushchev, who formed a conspiracy to overthrow him.

▼ Stalin lies in state, flanked by the men who would fight to succeed him (left to right): Khrushchev, Beria, Malenkov, Bulganin, Voroshilov and Kaganovich.

After winning over Molotov, Bulganin, Malenkov and six senior army officers, Khrushchev set a trap for Beria. On 26 June 1953, Beria walked unsuspectingly into a meeting at the Kremlin, where he was arrested by the conspirators. While Beria's bodyguards waited in the lobby, the police chief was himself smuggled out to an underground military bunker, where he was later shot.

Khrushchev had always been a loyal Stalinist yet, as leader of the Communist Party in the Ukraine, he had seen how unpopular Stalin's policies were. He believed that it was possible to do away with the worst features of Stalinism, such as the use of terror, and create a political system which would win the support of the Soviet people.

STALIN DENOUNCED

On 24 February 1956, Khrushchev made a devastating four-hour speech to the Twentieth Party Congress, in which he denounced Stalin for his personality cult, and for his use of terror against party members. Red Army General Dmitri Volgokonov described the reaction of Khrushchev's audience:

'I was stunned because I was a Stalinist... There was the silence of the grave reigning in the hall. When Khrushchev spoke, it was as though he were threading beads on to a string and adding more and more new facts, more and more criminal acts. Sometimes the hall buzzed with indignation, sometimes there were shouts of outrage and sometimes the hall was silent as a block of ice.'

UPRISING IN HUNGARY

Although Khrushchev's speech (see box) was meant to be for the party alone to hear, it was soon published abroad. In Hungary, Khrushchev's attack on Stalin encouraged the population to rise up against communism. On 1 November, the Hungarian leader, Imre Nagy, declared that his country had left the Soviet bloc. Khrushchev responded by sending in the Red Army, crushing the Hungarian uprising, and executing Nagy.

▼ Stalin's statue is smashed, during the short-lived Budapest uprising of October 1956. A crowd of 200,000 demonstrators marched through the streets, demanding freedom from Soviet rule.

The Hungarian uprising showed the difficulty of trying to reform the Communist system without the whole structure collapsing. Khrushchev was unable to solve this problem and, in 1964, he was overthrown by conservatives in the Soviet leadership. For the next two decades the system was presided over by the cautious Leonid Brezhnev, who resisted all demands for reform. Brezhnev was the first Soviet leader who did not even believe in the goals of communism. He said to his brother, 'All that stuff about Communism is a tall tale for popular consumption.'

NOSTALGIA FOR STALIN

As the Soviet system crumbled, many Communists looked back with nostalgia on Stalin, regretting Russia's lost superpower status. In 1990, Ivan Shekhovstsov, a retired lawyer, told a television interviewer:

'The respect I and the people of my generation feel for Stalin is based on the fact that he led for thirty years the first socialist state of workers and peasants. As Churchill said, when Stalin took Russia on, it had only the wooden plough, but he left it with nuclear weapons. At Stalin's death, Russia was one of the world's two most powerful states.'

THE FALL OF COMMUNISM

In 1985, Mikhail Gorbachev became general secretary of the Communist Party. Like Khrushchev, Gorbachev was a committed Communist, who thought that the system could work if only it was reformed to meet the needs of the people. He called for greater democracy and *glasnost* (openness), allowing freedom of speech for the first time since 1917. Gorbachev mistakenly thought that the party could control these reforms, underestimating just how unpopular it was. One after another, the Communist

▼ A demonstration by modern-day Russian supporters of Stalin, who look back fondly at the strong government he provided.

governments of eastern Europe were toppled. Finally, in 1991, the Soviet Union itself fell apart.

For some Communists, the fall of the Soviet Union led to a questioning of old beliefs. They had always thought that 'the ends justified the means'. But now that the ends, of building a communist paradise on earth, had been abandoned, they were forced to see the whole of Soviet history in a new light. Some, who had previously denounced Stalin for betraying Lenin's cause, now saw the cause itself as a tragic mistake. They also recognized that many of the features of Stalin's rule were already present in Lenin's leadership, including the suppression of opposing viewpoints, and the willingness to destroy entire social classes.

▲ A vast image of a modern Stalinist dictator, Saddam Hussein of Iraq.

STALIN THE ROLE MODEL

What made Stalin different from Lenin was his use of indiscriminate terror, and his personality cult. These two features of Stalinism are still with us, in countries like Iraq, where President Saddam Hussein uses a feared secret police to keep himself in power. Saddam's face is everywhere, looking down from vast posters. Like Stalin, he is shown in many different roles: as a general on top of a tank, a hero riding a white horse, or a kindly father-figure surrounded by smiling children.

Said Aburish is an Iraqi writer who knew Saddam Hussein in the 1970s, and later wrote a biography of him. This is how Aburish describes the influence of Stalin on the Iraqi dictator:

'Saddam Hussein models himself after Stalin more than any other man in history. He has a full library of books about Stalin. He reads about him, and when he was a young man – even before he attained any measure of power – he used to wander around... telling people, "Wait until I take over this country. I will make a Stalin state out of it yet!"

1878
6 DECEMBER
Joseph Dzugashvili born

1898
Russian Social Democratic
Workers' Party founded

1903
Social Democrats split into
Bolsheviks, led by Lenin,
and Mensheviks, led by Martov

1908–17
Dzugashvili arrested seven
times, spending long periods in
prison and exile

1911
Dzugashvili appointed to the
Central Committee of the
Bolshevik Party

1913
Dzugashvili adopts the
name 'Stalin'

1914
Beginning of First World War

1917
FEBRUARY
Workers strike and soldiers
mutiny in Petrograd
2 MARCH
Tsar Nicholas II abdicates
24–5 OCTOBER
Bolsheviks seize power

1918
JANUARY
Foundation of the Red Army
and beginning of the civil war
SUMMER
'War communism' introduced
AUGUST
'Red Terror', following an
assassination attempt on Lenin

1920
NOVEMBER
Last White Army defeated

1921
MARCH
Rising of Kronstadt sailors
against the Communist
government
Lenin announces the 'New
Economic Policy' allowing a
free market to flourish

1921–2
Famine

1922
APRIL
Stalin becomes
General Secretary
25 MAY
Lenin suffers first stroke

1924
Zinoviev, Kamenev and Stalin
in alliance against Trotsky
21 JANUARY
Death of Lenin

1925
JANUARY
Trotsky forced to resign from
the Commissariat of War

1926
Zinoviev and Kamenev ally with
Trotsky against Stalin. All three
are expelled from the Politburo

1928
JANUARY–FEBRUARY
Stalin forcibly takes grain from
the peasants
OCTOBER
First Five Year Plan for
industrialization begins

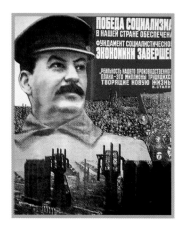

1929
APRIL
Defeat of Bukharin, who is
expelled from the Politburo
NOVEMBER
Stalin announces campaign of
collectivization and the
'liquidation of the kulaks'
DECEMBER
Stalin celebrates his 50th
birthday and launches his own
personality cult

1932
8 NOVEMBER
Stalin's wife Nadezhda
kills herself

1932–3
Famine in the Ukraine and the
North Caucasus

1934
1 DECEMBER
Murder of Sergei Kirov

1936
JULY
Beginning of the Spanish
Civil War
AUGUST
First great show trial, of
Zinoviev and Kamenev and
14 others
SEPTEMBER
Ezhov replaces Yagoda as head
of secret police

1937
JANUARY
Second great show trial, with
13 sentenced to death

MAY–JUNE
Purge of Red Army

1938
MARCH
Third show trial, of Bukharin,
Yagoda and 17 others

1939
23 AUGUST
Nazi–Soviet Pact signed
1 SEPTEMBER
Germany invades Poland
17 SEPTEMBER
Red Army invades Poland
30 NOVEMBER
Red Army invades Finland

1940
JUNE–AUGUST
Soviet Union takes over Baltic
States and part of Romania

1941
22 JUNE
Germany invades the
Soviet Union
DECEMBER
Red Army win first victory
over the *Wehrmacht*, just
outside Moscow

1942
AUGUST
Battle of Stalingrad begins

1943
2 FEBRUARY
Germans surrender at
Stalingrad
NOVEMBER–DECEMBER
Stalin meets Churchill and
Roosevelt at Tehran

1945
FEBRUARY
Stalin meets Churchill and
Roosevelt at Yalta
9 MAY
Red Army captures Berlin,
ending war in Europe

1946–50
Fourth Five Year Plan

1953
5 MARCH
Death of Stalin

1956
FEBRUARY
Khrushchev's secret speech
denouncing Stalin

1961
OCTOBER
Stalin's body removed from
Lenin's mausoleum

61

abdicate To formally give up power.
activists People who play an active role, especially in politics.
annex To take hold of territory.
anti-Semitism Hatred of Jews.

blitzkrieg 'Lightning war': a German method of warfare, using a concentration of firepower on a narrow front to advance quickly into enemy territory.
Bolsheviks The name for followers of Lenin from 1903 until 1918, when the Bolshevik Party became the Communist Party. Bolshevik means 'those of the majority'.
bureaucracy Government by officials, responsible only to their superiors.

cannibalism Eating human flesh.
capitalism An economic system based on private ownership of industries and services, and driven by the need to make profits.
Central Committee In theory, the governing body of the Communist Party, elected by party congresses and responsible for electing the Politburo. In practice, it was controlled by the Politburo.
collectivization The policy of making peasants give up their individual holdings and work on large-scale collective farms.
Comintern Communist International: the organization of international communist parties set up in 1919, and taking direction from the Soviet Union.
communism An economic system which aims to make everyone equal by abolishing private property, replacing it with common ownership.
conservatives People who are opposed to change.
co-operative A business in which individuals work together, pooling their resources and sharing the rewards.

coup The taking over and removal of a government by force.

defensive alliances Agreements between countries to help each other if they are attacked.
democracy Government by the people. In modern democracies, citizens' choose governments through elections.
demotion Moving someone to a lower position at work.
deported Forcibly sent abroad.
dictatorship Absolute rule. The Communists claimed to be ruling on behalf of the working class, and so they described their government as a 'dictatorship of the proletariat'.
diplomat Someone representing his or her government in dealings with a foreign government

exile A punishment in which someone is forced to leave his or her home or country.
expropriated Having had property taken away, usually by government order.

fascist A follower of the German Nazi Party, or any similar extreme nationalist political party.
free market Buying and selling without government interference, such as price fixing.

Gosplan State Central Planning Commission, responsible for directing the Soviet economy by creating targets for agricultural and industrial production.
GULAG Chief Administration for Corrective Labour Camps. The prison camps themselves came to be called the gulags.

industrialization The creation of new industries.
inflation Rising prices causing a fall in the value of money.

kulak Literally 'fist': an abusive name for a prosperous peasant farmer, able to employ farm labourers.

large-scale offensive An attack using large armies.
liberators Those who free people from unpopular rule or foreign occupation.
liquidation Wiping out or destroying.

Mensheviks The opponents of the Bolsheviks within the Social Democratic Party.
mobilize To prepare military forces for battle.
mutiny A revolt against authority in the armed forces. Soldiers and sailors mutiny when they refuse to obey their officers.

NKVD People's Commissariat for Internal Affairs: the name of the secret police from 1934 until 1946, when it became the MVD. The secret police was regularly renamed in an attempt to make it more popular.
non-aggression pact An agreement between countries not to fight each other.

peasants The poorest class of farmers.
personality cult An official policy of encouraging worship of a public figure.
piece-work wages Wages paid to a worker for each piece of work he or she produces.
Politburo Political Bureau. The policy-making body of the Communist Party.
politically aware Able to understand politics.
proletariat The Marxist name for the working class.
provisional government A temporary government, running a country in a period before elections are held.

revolutionary Someone aiming to bring about a complete change in society, usually through violence.
revolutionary underground A grouping of revolutionaries, forced by the law to live in hiding.

show trial A carefully managed legal trial, staged for political purposes.
socialism A theory of social organization in which the industries and services are owned and controlled by the community as a whole, rather than by individuals.
Soviet 'Council'. Soviets of workers and soldiers were set up during the revolution. They later became the basic unit of local government.
Soviet bloc Grouping of countries controlled by the Soviet Union.
superpower An extremely powerful state.

totalitarian A system of government which aims at complete control of the lives of citizens.
Tsar The title of the Russian emperor, derived from the Ancient Roman title, 'Caesar'.

unity Oneness. A country can be said to be united when people work together for a common cause.
USSR Union of Soviet Socialist Republics: the name of the Russian state from December 1922.

Vozhd 'Boss', the informal title for Stalin.

FURTHER INFORMATION

WEBSITES
The cyber USSR
http://www.tiac.net/users/hcun n/rus/index.html
Stalin's USSR lives on in cyberspace, at this witty but solidly factual site: 'a realm where no kulak goes unliquidated, no five-year-plan goes unoverfulfilled, and no Great Leader and Teacher goes unvenerated'.

Khrushchev's secret speech
http://home.uchicago.edu/~jab 3/index12.html
Full text of Khrushchev's 1956 speech denouncing Stalin.

Moscow trials 1936
http://art-bin.com/art/ omoscowtoc.html
The complete and incredible text of Stalin's show trial of Zinoviev and Kamenev.

BOOKS

For younger readers:
Stalin, Heinemann Leading Lives, 2000

Stewart Ross, *Causes of the Cold War*, Hodder Wayland, 2001
An exploration of the origins of US/Soviet rivalry.

For older readers:
Robert Conquest, *The Great Terror, A Reassessment*, Pimlico, 1992
A gripping account of the terror, from a historian who sees the whole process as planned in advance by Stalin.

J.Arch Getty and Oleg V.Naumov, *The Road to Terror: Stalin and the Self-Destruction of the Bolsheviks*, Yale University Press, 1999
This book uses recently released Russian documents to look at the wider causes of the terror, within the Communist Party. It shows an indecisive Stalin, switching from one political position to another.

Evgenia Ginzburg, *Into the Whirlwind*, Harvill, 1999
A moving account of one woman's experience of twenty years in Stalin's prison camps.

Alexander Solzhenitsyn, *The Gulag Archipelago*, Harvill, 1999
The classic book on Stalin's terror, by one of the greatest Russian writers of the twentieth century, using hundreds of personal testimonies from victims.